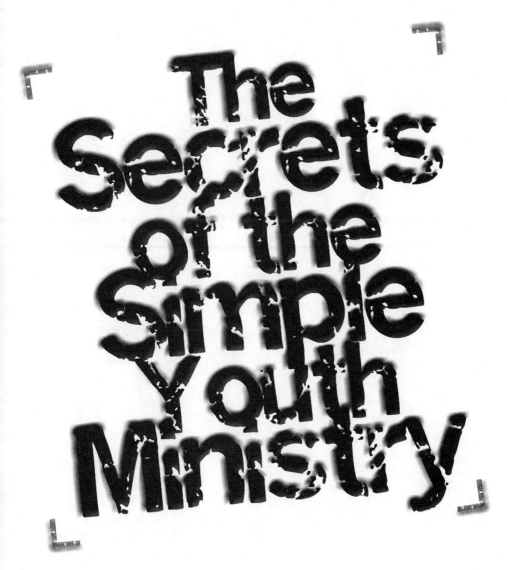

# The Secrets of the Simple Youth Ministry

## carl a. blunt

WINEPRESS WP PUBLISHING

Packaged by WinePress Publishing, PO Box 428, Enumclaw, WA 98022. The views expressed or implied in this work do not necessarily reflect those of WinePress Publishing. Ultimate design, content, and editorial accuracy of this work is the responsibility of the author.

ISBN 1-57921-350-2
Library of Congress Catalog Card Number: 00-110774

# ᚖTable of Contentsᚖ

**Introduction** ................................................................. xi

**Chapter One:** The Dream Begins ................................................. 13

**Chapter Two:** Reality Check ..................................................... 19

**Chapter Three:** Secret #1 . . . Ministry Community ................... 25

**Chapter Four:** Secret #2 . . . The Treasure ................................31

**Chapter Five:** Time Alone with God ...........................................39

**Chapter Six:** So Long, Hot Topics .............................................. 43

**Chapter Seven:** Ministry Design ................................................. 51

**Chapter Eight:** Secret #3 . . . Team-Based Ministry ................... 55

**Chapter Nine:** Secret #4 . . . The Target ................................... 63

**Chapter Ten:** The Midnight Sunrise ............................................71

**Epilogue:** Becoming a Youth Ministry Artist ........................... 75

**Study Guide**
    Ministry Community .........................................................78

    The Essential I's ............................................................... 80

    Treasure ..............................................................................84

    Christ as the Treasure of Your
        Ministry & Teaching .......................................................86

Christ as the Treasure of Ministry Design ........................... 88

Ministry Design Essentials ................................... 90

Team Ministry ........................................ 91

Target ................................................ 94

Dedicated to the Glory of God,
my wife Nikki, and children Taylor, Tanner, and Tate.

# Introduction to the Secrets of the Simple Youth Ministry

Having served in the youth ministry arena for well over a decade, I have seen fads, strategies, and programs come and go. The more youth ministry grows as a profession and an institution, the more complicated it becomes . . . especially for the volunteer youth workers representing the great majority of churches in the world.

Jesus never presented ministry or following Him as a complicated issue. He simply said, "Follow me." As the Executive Director of Christian Endeavor International, I have had the opportunity to speak with many youth workers around the world. What do they want and need? In a word: Simplicity.

I fully support the ongoing development of youth ministry studies, seminars, strategies, philosophies, and programs. All are valuable in the grand scheme of ministry to students. We need to return, however, to a simple way of doing ministry. I wrote this book and we created www.TeamCE.com to meet that need.

Remember Jesus' response when the teachers of the law asked Him to boil down His message? In Mark 12: 30–31, Jesus said it all came down to this. . . . Love God and love others. Simple. Jesus always made it simple . . . not easy, but simple.

Making youth ministry simple for you is the goal of this book. The Secrets of the Simple Youth Ministry is a fictional story based on true and lasting principles. I hope you enjoy and identify with the characters. I pray it will draw you into the loving arms of our Savior and release you to do His work in a simple way.

Simply His,
Carl Blunt

# ⮜Chapter One⮞
## The Dream Begins

Church emptied out earlier than usual and I arrived home by quarter after twelve. I quickly removed my sober church face, threw on some jeans and an old college sweatshirt, gathered some barbecue chips and soda, and flopped into my battered lazy boy. Time for some football? You bet. Remote in hand and body in chill mode, I found my favorite pre-game talking heads to fill me in on the action for the day. Sundays . . . definitely a day of rest for me. Normally by the beginning of the third quarter I'm fast asleep. Today was no different, but my dreams brought anything but relaxation. I held the position of Youth Leader at my church . . . not necessarily by choice. At least not my choice, but the Pastor's. I was young . . . teenagers are young. I had energy . . . teenagers have energy. I was single, in between jobs and school and without a life . . . they are single and need a life. Sounds like wisdom from God.

As I said, my dreams this particular Sunday were anything but peaceful. *The youth group meets every Sunday night from six until about seven-thirty.* As I fell into sleep mode, I found myself at the weekly youth group meeting. *None of my kids were there. In their place were about a dozen young men looking like guys auditioning for the part of Jesus in an Easter pageant. Dressed in their ragged first-century robes, they apparently were holding their own meeting. They did not notice me, so I stood quietly in the back and listened. "Why are people so attracted to our little gatherings? We don't have a cool building. The Romans have better, more exciting events. Why? Because we are a community . . . a Ministry Community. We share complete allegiance to a common Treasure. We are a team committed to loving and serving each other. We all stay focused on the same target. Unlike any other group . . . we are a Ministry Community."*

*As the speaker continued, my thoughts wandered. His description did not sound anything like my youth group or my church. In fact, our group was not even in the same ballpark. But, for some reason, it sounded much like the early church. It sounded much like what Christ desired of His Bride. It sounded much like what Christ desired of me.*

*"Jesus the Christ has captured and enraptured our hearts. He has made us His children. How great is the love the Father has lavished upon us that we should be called children of God. And that is what we are! We are His."*

*Silence. The moment seemed to last forever. I found myself caught in time as the speaker turned slowly, deliberately toward me. I could not escape his piercing gaze, as he looked deep inside of me. Our eyes locked, my lips quivering.*

*"You . . . you are His. Your little bunch is to be His bride . . . a Ministry Community."*

"TOUCHDOWN!"

I jumped from my seat, chips flew everywhere as the television announcer shocked me out of my sleep. My heart pounded and sweat poured from my brow. *Whoa! Where am I?* As I gathered myself from my fog, I noticed the clock. *Oh, no, it's nearly five o'clock and I have no plans for youth group.*

As I cleaned up the mess of chips, I racked my brain. *Sex, dating, relationships, drugs, alcohol, witness to your friends, etc. . .* Message after message danced through my mind. *What should I teach? What about a game? Maybe we could just have an hour and a half of silence. That sounds easy . . . and easy to justify. "Be still and know that I am God."* I had to find something. I decided to head off to church to check my shelves for some of those cool youth books— *Five Minutes to a Great Meeting* and *Don't Prepare, We Will.* They always work in a pinch. *I hope I haven't used them all,* I thought as I grabbed my coat.

I jumped in my excuse-for-a-car and rumbled off to church to get a "head start" on winging it at the meeting tonight. Every street sign during the ten-minute drive triggered an idea for a message or a theme for the night. *McDonald's golden arches reminds us of entering the golden gates. Burger King—Jesus is the King of all burgers.* As for a game, there was always volleyball, kickball, a combination of the two, or a variation of every game we have tried in the past.

As I pulled into the church driveway, another car caught my eye. It belonged to Rigdon, the new church janitor. *He must still be cleaning from the morning service. I had better act like I am thoroughly prepared for the youth meeting tonight.*

"Hi, Rigdon. Long day of cleaning?"

"Hey, Tanner. No, I finished cleaning hours ago. I was just here praying and waiting for you."

Startled and surprised, I could not respond.

"By the way, what are you teaching tonight?"

*Uh, oh. What was this, the janitor testing my preparedness for youth group?* I didn't think this was really any of his business.

"Well . . . last week we talked about serving one another. It went great. You know what? I really need to get going to make final preparations for tonight. See you later."

*I handled that one.* I headed to my office and the books that would save the day.

"Wait, Tanner . . ."

*Oh, no. Here he goes again.*

"How is your Ministry Community, anyway?"

*What? Ministry Community? Dream . . . Jesus look-a-likes.*

"My what?"

"Your Ministry Community," he said with a knowing smile.

*My dream . . . strange coincidence . . . strange phrase.*

"Strange."

"What's strange?" Rigdon asked.

"Where did you hear the phrase, 'Ministry Community'?"

"From a janitor in my old church. I volunteered as youth leader there before I moved here to care for my aging mother. B.Z., the janitor, taught me the *Secrets of the Simple Youth Ministry*. It begins with the idea of a youth group as a Ministry Community."

"Sounds interesting, but I really have to come up with something for tonight . . . I mean finish preparing for tonight. Maybe we can talk later. See you." I nearly ran to my office.

*Secrets of the Simple Youth Ministry? What is that?* Sounded like some Gnostic or New Age philosophy for reaching the "inner selves" of teenagers to me. *I think I will stick with Youth Specialties and Group.*

I opened the box on my desk as I settled down to develop a brilliant plan. *A video—that would be easy. We could watch a video and discuss it. I think we even have some popcorn and soda somewhere.* I took a video off the shelf. *Cool, this video includes a discussion guide. This is going to be a piece of cake. No need for a game, the video is an hour long. This is great!*

I set up the youth room for the video, cooked some popcorn, and laid out the beverages for the evening. I had planned a great night—so I thought.

Unfortunately, like every other Sunday night youth group for months, the meeting was lifeless. Teenagers were there physically, but in another world spiritually. We interrupted the video several times to quiet the crowd. The discussion time consisted of me asking questions, students making jokes, and me providing the answers to the questions. I felt thoroughly demoralized. Another night, another failure. *I need to get into another business*, was my only thought.

"Hi," Rigdon showed up at the youth room. I waved to acknowledge his presence and kept on cleaning.

"How did it go tonight?"

I shrugged my shoulders in obvious disappointment.

"Maybe I could help. I'd love to sit down and talk about the *Secrets of the Simple Youth Ministry* sometime."

"Yeah. Sounds great." *Yeah, right. How can you possibly help me?* I thought.

"How about tonight?"

"I'm kind of tired. Maybe some other time."

"Tomorrow?"

*This guy won't let up.* "Sure," knowing I could get out of this later.

"Tomorrow at eleven a.m. in your office."

"Why not." Monday was my day off. I could conveniently forget our meeting.

"See you later. I'm praying for you, Tanner."

"Thanks." I shrugged the old man off and went home deflated.

# ⌒Chapter Two⌒
## Reality Check

Another restless night, but I knew tomorrow would prove to be a great day. I had tickets to the afternoon baseball game in the middle of a hot and heavy pennant race. Tomorrow would be *my* day.

I love to sleep and the clock read ten o'clock before I saw the light of day. Time to get some breakfast, watch some morning game shows, and head off to the game. After "The Price is Right," a shower, and some cereal, I ran into a slight problem . . . the tickets. I could not find the tickets anywhere. *Oh yeah, I stuck them in my Bible.* I searched for it by my coat that I had thrown off the night before. *I must have left it at the church.*

I finished getting ready and sped off to the church to pick up my tickets. *Good, Rigdon's not here*, I observed as I pulled in the driveway. *I'll get in and out in a flash.* I grabbed my Bible laying on the middle of my desk.

Knock! Knock! Knock!

"Hello!"

*Rigdon!* I looked at my watch. Eleven o'clock! I stood trapped with no way out.

"Have a seat," I resigned myself to the fact that this "chat" would happen one way or another.

"You have the floor. Fill me in on these *Secrets of The Simple Youth Ministry*."

"Let's go for a walk outside."

We walked in silence for a couple minutes through the trees surrounding the church. In the distance I could hear the chatter of children playing a game of kickball at the nearby school playground. *Children playing, no cares or worries . . . just laughter—how refreshing,* I thought.

"Tell me about your group, Tanner." Rigdon broke the silence.

I sighed heavily. *Hey, I thought I was the student and the old janitor the teacher.* Wrong again.

"Well, I guess you could say we are a typical youth group. We have our weekly meeting with games, some teaching, music, and just hanging-out time. Every month we go to concerts and other events that give my students opportunities to bring their friends. Our group seems to like each other at church, but doesn't hang out together much outside the church walls. Some kids like to come. Many don't come, don't care, and don't care when they do come. Typical."

"Too bad. No offense, but that doesn't sound like the church, the Bride, that Jesus called us to be."

"Yeah, but I've tried just about everything that has come down the pike. Youth Ministry modeling the life of *Jesus, Purpose-Led Youth Ministry, Competition-based Youth Ministry, etc . . .* I've tried it all. And sure it works to some extent, but . . ."

"How do you measure whether or not a program works?"

"You know, numerical growth, interest in spiritual things, etc, etc . . ."

"Did Jesus use those measurements? Did he ever cajole anyone into following Him?"

"What do you mean?"

Rigdon pointed toward the playground. "How many of those kids woke up today expecting not to go to school? Probably none. Why? School is life to an elementary student. They learn, grow, meet friends, and plan their futures at school. Kids consider everything outside of school as 'extra-curricular.' School time is viewed as the 'curriculum'."

"And . . . go on," the old man had my attention.

"The point is that we tend to think of a typical youth group as an 'extra-curricular' choice for Christian teenagers. We really view youth group no differently than music, sports, or Boy Scouts. Except that parents often force their kids to go to youth group."

Now Rigdon really had my attention as he continued. "A Ministry Community, Tanner, is seen differently. It is *the* curriculum, or the main event in a member's life. Everything else is 'extra-curricular'. You can call any group of teens a 'youth group', but a Ministry Community exists for ministry."

"It's still kind of fuzzy to me," I said as Rigdon paused. "Please go on." The old sage's words were definitely interesting, but I did not want to be disappointed by another 'youth program'.

The janitor stopped and looked directly at me, "A Ministry Community becomes the 'norm' for its members while everything else is just that . . . everything else. The early church had no 'program' for evangelism or any other type of program for that matter. They functioned simply as a living, breathing organism with three distinctions. First, they shared a complete allegiance to a common Treasure. Second, they worked as a team committed to loving and serving each other. And third, they all focused on the same target. Unlike any other group. . . they were a Ministry Community."

"Sounds great, but how do I accomplish this?"

"What time is it?"

I looked at my watch, "Eleven-thirty. Oh, no! I need to get going. I have tickets to the game in the city today."

"Tell you what, Tanner, I want you to just sit back and think for a while. Think about the differences between a typical youth group and a Ministry Community. Evaluate your group and events. Just think, think, think. We'll talk again soon."

"Sure. Thanks. See you later." I felt unsure of what that little talk was about. *Think?* Youth ministry is about doing, not thinking. Whatever . . . maybe I'll give it some thought later. He painted a pretty picture . . . pretty unrealistic. I brushed it off and ran to the game.

Or at least I tried to brush it off. The game was a blur. I could not get the idea of a Ministry Community out of my mind. The early church was a force to be reckoned with. My church, especially my youth group, acted like a force you could ignore, if even a force at all. No one was on the same page; they were half-committed to Christ and less committed to each other. I watched the game, half through wandering thoughts and half in a daze. As the game progressed, I began to see something. I noticed the precision with which the ballplayers on the field worked together to make a simple play in the field. Pitcher to catcher, hit to shortstop, throw to first—batter is out. They all wanted to win and they all played to win. They shared a common goal.

"Hotdogs! Get your hotdogs here!"

Nothing like a stadium hotdog to bring a dreamer back to reality.

"I'll take one," I called to the vendor.

*Great, so much for a day off as Youth Leader.* The hotdog vendor was Tate Allen, a loner who wanders into our youth group when he feels like it.

"Hey, Tate," turning on the youth leader charm and forcing every ounce of amiability I could muster.

"Hi, Tanner," Tate answered.

"How are hotdog sales today?"

"Okay," he shrugged.

*Typical teenage answer—no details,* I mused to myself. "We missed you at youth group last night." I attempted to drag more out of him.

"Yeah, couldn't make it."

"We'd love to see you there next week."

"Maybe. I might have to work." He quickly pasted stadium mustard on my foot-long and turned to fill orders from the rows below us. Nodding my direction, he muttered, "Later, man."

"Hope to see you next week."

Kids like Tate drive me nuts. I love them to death, but their lack of interest is enough to make me quit. I focused my attention back on the game.

Bottom of the ninth, score tied 0-0, two outs, my favorite pitcher stalking the mound. The pitch, the crack of the bat, the flight . . . "back, back, back, back, back . . ." I could hear Chris Berman now, calling the game highlights. Home run, we lose.

# ⟨Chapter Three⟩
## Secret #1 . . . Ministry Community

The rest of the week was typical. A junior high sporting event, a high school band concert, a complaint from a parent that the yearly schedule is not together yet. "How can you expect us to plan for youth events if we don't even know when they're coming? Blah . . . blah . . . blah . . . blah . . ."

Sunday night came and went. Dull, lifeless, same stuff, different night. *Ministry Community, yeah, right.* I had not seen Rigdon since Monday, but his words bugged me the whole week. Later I found out that he had taken his mother to visit her sister upstate. Was it possible to create a Ministry Community? If so, I needed to know how.

On Tuesday, after a restful day off, I looked for Rigdon, but he was still gone. By now this "Ministry Community" thing was driving me crazy. I needed answers. God called me to minister to teenagers, but I felt worn out. I hung on at the end of my rope. I was ready for any plan that might come close to creating the kind of group that Rigdon told me about.

Wednesday morning brought administrative stuff and a light-hearted staff meeting. The pastor had plans that night and needed someone to lead the prayer meeting. I quickly went into the famous grade school "please-don't-call-on-me-while-I-refuse-to-make-eye-contact" pose. Wednesday night prayer at our church felt like "The Night of the Living Dead."

I hurried out of the meeting, knowing full well that Pastor would be on my heels, making one of his patented one-on-one pleas for me to lead the prayer meeting. As God in His mighty providence would have it, I ran into Rigdon on the way out of the meeting. I was safe . . . at least for a few minutes.

"Hi, Rigdon. How was your trip?" I asked.

"Refreshing. I had a nice drive through the countryside and my mother enjoyed her visit."

"Good. Well, I've been looking for you. I'd like to . . ."

"Ministry Community, right?"

*Man, this guy is good. How did he know? Strange things were happening.*

"Well . . . yeah . . . I'm just curious." I did not want to sound too anxious for his help. After all, I did okay with the youth ministry . . . sort of.

Just then, Pastor came out of his office looking for me.

"Hi, Rigdon. I didn't realize you were back. How was your trip?"

"Nice and refreshing."

"Well, it's great to see you again. You know, I'm going to be out of town tonight."

*Here he goes . . . sensing the perfect opportunity and moving in for the kill.*

To my amazement, Pastor turned to Rigdon. "I remember you mentioning something about leading the prayer meeting sometime. How would you like to lead it tonight?"

Inside, my heart jumped for joy. *I hate leading the prayer meeting . . . and Rigdon wants to? Strange bird, this Rigdon fellow.*

"I'd be glad to lead the meeting," Rigdon beamed.

*Yes!* I turned to walk away, flashing a quick Tiger Woods fist pump. *I'm off the hook.*

"Do you mind if I spend a few moments talking about how we can become more of a Ministry Community?" Rigdon said it loud enough for me to hear as I walked away.

*There's that phrase again.*

"Sure." Pastor held no concern about content; he just wanted to make sure someone took care of Wednesday night prayer meeting.

Of course I attended, tempted by Rigdon's bait.

The prayer meeting began with a few announcements about some weekend activities for the older people. The seniors in our church were very active, always going on trips and other events. They put the younger crowd to shame.

"Friends, all of you know me. I'm Rigdon, the janitor. But you may not know that I used to be very involved in the youth ministry at my previous church. I held the position of Youth Leader for ten years.

"I would like to share with you one simple concept that transformed my ministry. An 82-year-old gentleman named B.Z. shared this idea with me. If you will indulge me a few minutes, I believe that, if we catch this simple principle, it could transform the life of our church."

Rigdon had me on the edge of my seat. I am not sure why, but I felt confident that God planned to use this moment. I knew that if He didn't, I was ready to quit youth ministry.

Everyone's eyes were fixed on Rigdon as he spoke. "My first year leading the youth ministry of Apple Creek Community Church was frustrating. The youngsters did not listen, did not come, and did not participate when they did come. I tried many different types of curriculum. I even went to a few seminars that I paid for myself. To make a long story short . . . I wanted to quit and let someone else take over, except for one slight problem—no one else wanted the job. I felt stuck."

*Yeah, I am with you all the way, Rigdon. I know the feeling. But cut the small talk and get to the answers.*

As if he could read my mind Rigdon said, "Let me share with you how I came to know about creating a Ministry Community. Our church had a well-respected, quiet man named B.Z. He was a spry old man, full of energy and excitement. Every week I would see him talking with visitors, sharing his life stories with regulars, and helping others simply feel welcome. Everyone loved B.Z.

"Well, one day after a youth meeting, he noticed that I was a bit down. 'Things not going well with the youth ministry?' he asked me.

"I told him how I was ready to give up and he asked me if I had ever heard of a Ministry Community. Of course, I hadn't. And B.Z. just said, 'Let's go for a ride.' Well, I had nothing to lose so I went with B. Z. He took me in his old 1981 Cadillac that rode like a charm."

*Enough about the car—get to the point.* "Tanner, be patient," I told myself. *Rigdon is a storyteller, not a journalist.*

Rigdon went right on with his story, "As we rode, B.Z. painted me a picture of the early church, based on Acts 2:42. He taught me that the early church was more than a group of people with like interests who met together for a good time. They were more than people who shared some similar convictions. They were more than people who liked each other's company. They were a community.

"I didn't quite get his point at first. Every local town calls itself a community. B. Z. explained the difference between a youth group and a Ministry Community by sharing his experiences working with a Christian Endeavor youth group, the first youth ministry in America. B.Z. recalled what made CE a Ministry Community.

"First, he said that a community involves life-sharing at the deepest levels, based on our unity and whole-life commitment to Jesus Christ. It is more than having acquaintances and friends. It is truly having brothers and sisters. . .being a family. Not just a family in name, but in practice. B.Z. gave me an example of a shared Christ-life from his own experience.

"One summer the local factory laid off his dad. B.Z.'s family ran out of money and became way behind on the rent. Two families that attended their neighborhood church shared a deep commitment to Christ. During B.Z.'s family struggles, these two families did more than say, 'We'll pray for you.' They entered into their brothers' and sisters' struggles and helped carry them through. They chipped in and shared their Christ-life in every way. They provided money and time. They watched the kids while B.Z.'s mom worked some odd jobs, and helped his dad find odd jobs. They shared the burdens of life because their 'family' was hurting and needy. These families willingly made sacrifices in order to help.

"They also shared the successes. When B.Z.'s dad finally got a job, they threw a neighborhood party to celebrate God's faithfulness. His dad tried to pay back the other two families, but they would not take a dime, citing the passage where Jesus said to give without expecting any in return."

*Wow! That must have been a cool neighborhood. I would sure love to live there.*

Rigdon went on, calmly sharing the principles of the Ministry Community. "A shared Christ-Life is essential to creating a Ministry Community. It's also important that this community focus on ministry, both to those inside and to those outside. Oh my . . ." Rigdon glanced at the clock on the wall. "We'd better get down to prayer. I've gone a little long. Maybe I can share more later."

*Sure . . . more later. Maybe everyone else was fine with that, but that won't work for me.* Time was running out and I still wanted to throw in the towel. Everything Rigdon said sounded great. But, number one, he did not say anything new. And, number two, he did not say much. But what he did say, I wanted for my youth ministry.

*I desperately want my kids to become a Ministry Community, sharing the Christ-life together. But how? They have no interest in sacrificing for anyone but themselves. They have baby-tree roots with weak branches for their faith. I wish God would just step in and make my group a Ministry Community. He parted the Red Sea. Why can't He just do a "Ministry Community miracle" in my group?*

The rest of the prayer meeting finished with the usual small talk mixed with prayer. Some prayers would have topped the publican on the street corner for their piety and pride. Others were short and sweet, full of gratitude and thanksgiving. I remained lost in thought and simply passed the time, wanting to take Rigdon for a ride in *my* car this time.

After the meeting, I made my way to the front to speak with Rigdon.

"Rigdon, want to go for a ride?"

He just smiled his knowing smile and lifted his hand to the door, directing me to lead the way.

# ⤳Chapter 4⤳
## Secret #2 . . . The Treasure

This time it was my turn. I had him in my rusty 1993 Ford Escort and he was not getting away until I felt satisfied or we were taken to heaven.

"Okay, Rigdon. Let me see here, a Ministry Community has a shared Christ-life as opposed to being a bunch of individual Christians each with his or her own walk, right?"

"You're catching on, Tanner. We live in a culture that thrives on individualism and independence. We are Americans. We fix our own problems and keep it to ourselves. But, you see, that runs contrary to the call of Jesus to depend on God and to share each other's burdens. God called us to be a community, not a group of individuals."

"I think I'm getting it." I was starting to see the picture, but I had a long way to go and I needed one of *Paul's* famous milkshakes.

"How about a trip to *Paul's Diner*? I'm buying."

"Sounds great."

As we drove, Rigdon began to share his frustrations with Christians not connecting with each other, but choosing to do their own thing on their own time. He said that individualism hurt the church, especially our ability to show the world how much we love each other. He shared about the potential impact of others seeing Christians who love each other in words and actions. He even raised his normally quiet voice in excitement as he talked about the 3,000 added in one day in the book of Acts.

*Paul's* only had a few customers, so the waitress took our orders right after we sat down. I listened intently to Rigdon until our orders came. After a quick sip of my milkshake, I began my line of questioning.

"So, I'm with you, Rigdon. I think what you're talking about sounds great. No argument here. That is obviously God's plan. My real question is . . ."

"Let me guess . . . HOW?"

I shook my head and smiled. He always seemed to know my thoughts and finish my sentences. My mom and dad used to do that to me when I was a little boy. I hated it then, but Rigdon had a way about him that drew me in. His knowing smile reminded me of my father's gentle moments of concern for me as a teenager.

"Yes . . . how," I laughed. "How do I create a Ministry Community in my youth group?"

"It begins with you."

"What do you mean?"

"Well, youth ministry from a leadership perspective boils down to modeling and teaching. In teaching, we share why we do something and maybe some pointers on how we do it. But modeling is a real-life picture of how to live it. It's like watching a video. Let's talk about modeling first. When was the last time you were involved in sharing your Christ-life with other believers?"

Ouch! That hurt. My countenance fell as I looked away, deep into my milkshake, trying to avoid eye contact with Rigdon. I wanted help with my youth ministry, not personal attacks. But, I guess I would not feel guilty if I had nothing to feel guilty about. Rigdon hit the nail on the head. Sharing my Christ-life? I hardly had a Christ-life to share. I opened my Bible when I had to prepare a message or find an answer for a teenager. Daily devotions consisted of a quick, "God, thanks for the day" prayer and sometimes a quick verse. My passion for Christ hid behind my frustration for ministry.

"Hmm. Maybe I should ask first about your own Christ-life. How are things between you and Jesus?"

"Well . . . it's not been smooth sailing lately. He seems distant, but I know it's me who has moved. I miss Him. I've been running on empty for awhile now."

"Now is the time to change that, Tanner. Ask God to give you a burning desire to know Him and a passion to dig deep into His mind through His Word."

"Yeah, that's what I want." I took another deep sip of my milkshake, lamenting the past few months of missed time with my Savior. I cried out to Him in my heart, begging, pleading for Him to give me a passion for Him. *God, help me breathe deeply of Your grace and mercy.*

"Hello . . . Tanner, are you still there?"

It seemed like fifteen minutes had passed since we last spoke. I had business with God to tend to. Oblivious to Rigdon's presence, I drank deeply the open-armed grace of my Father.

"Sorry about that. I kind of checked out for a few."

"I know . . . taking care of business," he said with his knowing smile and a wink.

"So, it starts with me. What about me?"

"Well, there are three main areas we need to talk about."

I desired to hear it, but I did not buy him a milkshake to talk about me. I wanted answers about my youth ministry, but off he went.

"First, we need to talk about your identity. Tell me about yourself."

"Well, I love Cheerios. I don't understand how Wheaties ever became the breakfast of Champions. Cheerios gets my vote. I also love pizza. Thin crust, loaded with cheese and. . . ."

"That's not what I mean," laughed Rigdon. "Where were you before you met Christ? What spiritual state were you in?"

"Well, I was a sinner, just like everyone else. A sinner, in need of a Savior."

"You mean a sinner running from, and battling with, the Savior. You see, Romans 5:10 says that before we knew Christ, we were at war with Him. We wanted nothing to do with Him."

I nodded and continued, "One night, Christ found me, a teenager lost and alone, searching for a way home. He forgave me of my sins and adopted me into His family."

"Amazing isn't it?" Rigdon chimed in. "One minute you are a sinner bound for the terrible wrath of a holy God, the next minute you sit as His child, wrapped in His blood-stained grace."

"Where are we going with this?"

"Well, the first thing you need to model is your identity in Christ. You are a child of God. 1 John 3:1 says: 'How great is the love the Father has lavished upon us that we should be called children of God. And that is what we are.'"

Rigdon sipped some ice water and continued.

"Never forget who you are, Tanner. Rest in your identity. Your security in Christ is based on what He did for you, not what you did, or will do, for Him. Stop worrying about results in your youth ministry. Results are God's job. Our job is simply to be faithful. Relax, God is in complete control."

I leaned back in my seat. "Rigdon, that's refreshing to hear. Most of the time I hear about numbers and growing my group."

"Do you remember a passage in the book of John where John the Baptist's disciples wondered what he thought about everyone leaving him to go with Jesus?" I nodded. "John told his disciples, 'A man can receive only what is given him from heaven.' God will take care of the numbers; you simply be faithful to His call on your life."

"Okay, identity. I won't forget who I am. What's next?"

The waitress interrupted our conversation, "Would you guys like something else? We'll be closing in ten minutes."

It was getting late, but I was not going to let Rigdon go until I picked his brain some more. My life and ministry changed as we spoke.

"No, thanks. Rigdon, do you mind if we continue this conversation at the county reservoir? I have a spot there where I go to think on nights like this."

"Well, I should check in on my mother to make sure she's okay."

After paying our bill and a quick phone call, we were off again, rattling down the road in my "youth leader special." On the way to the reservoir, Rigdon began to explain the second important element for living as a good model before the teenagers. "First is Identity, next is Intimacy. God desires a deeply intimate relationship with each of His children. He desires constant communion with us."

This was all new to me. Most seminars and books I read talked mainly about techniques and tricks for youth ministry, not about me being right with God.

I parked at my favorite spot and we stepped out of the car. Rigdon began sharing about his relationship with Christ. Even in the dark, I could see that his eyes lit up and his voice was full of excitement.

"Jesus and I have been together for nearly twenty years now. There have been some ups and downs, but I can honestly say that I grow more passionately in love with Him every day. We have a deeply intimate relationship that affects every area of my life."

That sounded great. It was certainly something I was missing, something I longed for but never knew I could have.

Rigdon leaned against the front of the car and I sat on the hood. He had my undivided attention as he continued, "Do you remember the passage in Psalm 139 about 'where can we go to escape from His presence'?"

"Yeah, I always thought that meant that God is everywhere and we can't escape Him or His judgment."

"True, but that Psalm also talks about the pursuit of a passionate love, our passionate loving Father. He constantly seeks us and desires to spend time with us. In fact, verses 17 and 18 teach that God's thoughts for us outnumber all the sands on all the seashores."

"Wow! That's good stuff. I need to share that with my teenagers."

"First, you need to experience it."

"You're right," I sighed and raised my hands to the sky, "Here I am, Lord. Teach me."

I could not believe my ignorance of God's grace and love toward me. I had been a Christian for nearly five years. I thought I knew it all. I could quote Scripture, tell the great stories of the faith, sing the great hymns and new choruses, and pray with the best of them. Motions . . . just motions. For too long I had just gone through the motions. Now it was time to experience my faith.

"Intimacy with Jesus. I want it, Rigdon. How do I get it?"

"Seek Him."

I waited patiently for him to say more. I waited. . .

"And . . ."

"Seek Him with all your heart, soul, mind, and strength. Spend time with Him in prayer, listen to His heart through Scripture, think about Him all throughout the day, set your gaze upon Him."

"Okay." It all sounded a bit strange, but I was willing to give it a try.

Rigdon wasn't finished yet. "Identity—know who you are in Christ; Intimacy—know that He pursues you and you need to passionately pursue Him. And the third thing—Integration."

"Integration? Sounds like Math class."

"Integration simply means living the Christ-life throughout every area of your life."

My mind wandered as I considered the implications of Rigdon's words. He talked on and on about "washing dishes for Jesus" and doing "everything to the glory of God." *I thought following Christ was just about Bible study, church, prayer, and stuff. Now he says that my entire life must be transformed and I need to take on the "mind of Christ" in all things. I have to consider how my faith impacts my work, my thoughts, my speech, my relationships, my television viewing habits, and . . . everything!*

I wanted to run from this reality. "Rigdon, it's getting late and I've got to get home."

"Sure. One last question. Tanner, is Christ the Treasure of your life?" Rigdon raised his hand toward me. "Don't answer now. Take some time over the next few days and compare Paul's words in Philippians 3:4–11 with your life. Paul found his Treasure, have you? Let me pray for you before we go."

After an intense prayer time where Rigdon seemed to really connect with God on my behalf, we jumped in my car and drove away. I could not help but dwell on Rigdon's challenge to integration. My life was anything but integrated. I lived life in different compartments. I had a work compartment, a home compartment, a church compartment, etc. . . all disconnected. I put on different faces for different places and different people. Before I even dropped him off, I felt a wave of depression. I had a long way to go to an integrated life.

# ⇜Chapter Five⇝
## Time Alone with God

My meeting with Rigdon made it clear that changes in my own life were long overdue. I decided to take vacation days on the following Thursday and Friday for a mini-retreat with just God and me. A quick phone call to the director of our local summer camp, provided arrangements for me to spend a few days in one of their cabins deep in the woods. Although I like camping, I also enjoy the creature comforts of my apartment. These few days at Camp Shiloh would challenge me, but that was okay. I did not want any distractions . . . just God and me.

I packed a few things, like my football, my thinking tool. Toss it up, catch it. Toss it up, catch it. Over and over again. I did my best thinking with that old football. No books, but my Bible. It had been a long time since I had seriously meditated on God's thoughts and actions.

On the way to the camp, I prayed that God would use this time as a refreshing experience, but more than that I wanted Him to reveal His heart and show me His will. I prayed, *God, I want to meet with You. For the next two days—just You and me. Let this time away from television, sports, internet, phone and most of all—people, open my heart once again to You.*

The first day was hard and long. God's hand seemed to make time stand still. I felt withdrawals from the world as I walked around the camp tossing my football up in the air. As I walked across the softball field, my mind went back to my conversation with Rigdon.

*Intimacy . . . I am probably more intimate with this football than I am with God!* I punted the ball toward the outfield.

Stuffing my hands in my pocket, I felt sullen and depressed. I walked to pick up my football and headed toward the high ropes course. *Maybe if I climb higher I can get closer to God,* I reasoned.

I spent most of the rest of the day sitting on the wooden perch, fifty feet above the ground. From there I could see most of the camp. As I soaked in the quiet and peacefulness of the surroundings, my black cloud started to lift. A rabbit scurried across the field. I began to talk to God. *Okay, Lord, I want to become intimate with You. I want to know Your will in all things. I don't want to toss You aside like my football and pick You up when I need You. Please Lord, help me to draw closer to You.*

A small herd of deer cautiously came out of the nearby woods and started grazing in the field below me. The large buck occasionally sniffed the air to check for signs of danger. My presence caught his attention and he stared at me for several minutes. I didn't move a muscle and he soon realized I was harmless. A chestnut doe nudged her straying fawn closer to the herd. *Identity . . . each member has his or her own identity within the herd. Rigdon is right, Lord. My identity lies in You. How could I take for granted what You did for me? Why have I been trying so hard to find my identity in what I think I am doing for You? It doesn't matter if I'm some big hot shot youth leader. What matters is what You did for me . . . not what I do for You.*

I took a deep breath and soaked in the beauty of Creation and realized for the first time how beautiful the Creator is. I recalled how God gave me identity when He broke my chains of sin. Remembering my first love refreshed me like a free-falling waterfall and I began to feel intimacy with God again.

Dusk came and the deer had returned to the forest, so I grabbed my football and climbed from my heavenward perch. I walked back across the campgrounds tossing the ball into the air, but this time not to think. I now did my thinking with God. The full moon gave enough light for a night hike along the camp's nature path. As I sauntered along the wooded trail, God continued to work a heart transformation, breaking me and putting me back together over and over. He showed me that although my motives may have been wrong for taking the position of youth leader—something to fill the void—it was no accident. God had called me to this job for a purpose. He convicted me of my wasted time in front of the television and not spending time with Him. No wonder I had no idea about intimacy with God. I felt convicted that the time had come to integrate my entire life with Him. The trees sometimes hid the moon and the trail darkened and I realized how often other things blocked God's light in my life.

Before I knew it, I found myself at the outdoor chapel at the end of the trail. It stood in a clearing and the moon rose high in the sky, shining the way to the shelter. Emotion erupted in my soul and I ran to the large wooden cross at the bottom of the natural amphitheater. Collapsing in a pile at the foot of the cross, I cried out, "Here am I! Use me, Lord! Send me! Break me!" I wept until my exhausted body could take no more.

The morning sunlight felt warm as I woke the next morning, still at the foot of the cross. My body ached from lying on the cool ground all night, but my soul felt exhilarated. I stretched my arms to the sky and said aloud, "Lord, if You want me to stick it out in youth ministry, I am Your willing servant. From now on I leave the specifics up to You!"

I jumped up and headed back to the main campgrounds. Now my stomach rumbled from hunger. Food was the farthest thing from my mind when I packed my gear. I planned to thrive on spiritual bread, but now I felt hungry from the wrestling with God the day before. *The mess hall, surely there is something left behind.* I headed toward the camp kitchen. The director had given me a set of keys to every main building so I let myself in and started foraging like a mouse. *Yes! Peanut butter and crackers and a box of Cheerios—the mainstay of life!* A little bit of a dry meal, but it tasted like a feast.

I grabbed the box of cereal and started nibbling as I walked around the large mess hall. A large bulletin board caught my attention. I needed something to read with my Cheerios since I had no morning comics. The words *Simple Youth Ministry—Turn Your Group into a Ministry Community!* caught my attention. I pulled a flyer off the board. *There's that phrase again!* I read the brochure, *Christian Endeavor will show you how to turn your youth ministry into a community.* I munched on some more Cheerios. *Christian Endeavor...where have I heard that name before? Rigdon! That guy follows me everywhere!*

The brochure gave the name of a new program called TeamCE. It provided a three-year systematic plan for making youth groups into ministry communities. The flyer listed their website, www.TeamCE.com, and promised youth leaders that they could find everything they needed to run their youth ministries. Then I sensed that the hand of the Lord had led me to the camp and to the mess hall. *Thank You, Lord, You are so faithful. Thank You for giving me the next step.*

I spent the next day on long walks with my Savior, talks with my Lover, moments of reading and meditating on His eternal words, and periods of silence listening for His "still small voice." Restoration is the only way I can describe the miraculous time with God. For the first time in my ministry—in my Christian life—I was ready for God to do the work and for me to simply be His tool.

# ⮜Chapter Six⮞
## So Long, Hot Topics

Saturday morning I returned to find Rigdon sitting on my door-step.

"Hey, Tanner! How was your time with God?"

*Funny . . . I don't recall telling Rigdon that I planned to go on a retreat.* "Rigdon, what are you doing here? And, by the way, how did you know where I was?"

"Well, my friend, I'm here to help you walk a little further down the path to the *Simple Youth Ministry*," he said with his now-familiar grin. To most people it may have seemed like an arrogant smirk, but I knew full well his grin came from fulfillment deep in his soul from helping me with my life and ministry.

"Great, but how did you know where I was?"

"What do you mean?" Rigdon asked with a puzzled look. "Where were you?"

"You just asked me about my time with God. I just spent two days alone with Him at Camp Shiloh."

"Great. There is nothing like time alone with the Father to bring new vision and passion to life and ministry."

Every time I met with this guy, he confused me more. How did he know that I had just spent time with God? I prepared myself for Rod Serling to step in and explain my entrance into the Twilight Zone.

"How did you know . . .?"

"Remember when Moses came down from the mountaintop?"

"Yeah," I replied, thinking, *What does that have to do with anything?*

"Your face, your smile. You look well rested, refreshed. Nothing brings that kind of renewal but time with God."

*Strange fellow, this Rigdon character.* I kept my real thoughts silent and asked, "What were you thinking that we might do today?"

"A trip to the local nature preserve to hear Dr. Maxwell talk about the local wildlife."

*I think I will say it again . . . this guy is really strange.* Now I *really* wanted to let Rigdon know what I *really* thought. I had little interest in nature and wildlife. I enjoyed a trip to the zoo once a year just like everyone else, but . . . a lecture on wildlife in the Midwest? "Rigdon, I don't know about that. Any other ideas? I'm not sure how much time I have today. I've got some work to do after being out of the loop for the past two days," muddling my way out of the Jane and Tarzan lecture.

"I already told Dr. Maxwell that I would attend and bring a friend."

*Now he is planning my life.* Last week I was a struggling youth leader with no real direction, drowning in frustration. This week I am still confused, but refreshed. The frustration has been replaced by a new sense of hope and optimism for my life and ministry. I had the "X" Factor to thank for that—a little old church janitor. Even if Rigdon was planning my life, it was working. Besides, I had nothing better to do on this beautiful Saturday morning—except sleep and regroup from my "retreat."

"I guess I have no choice, do I?" I said with a smile. "You have it all planned out, don't you?"

"Put your stuff inside and let's go."

In the car, I shared about my time at the camp. Rigdon listened intently, taking every opportunity to nod and show his approval. It felt unnerving at times, but I always knew he wanted to pay close attention. That cannot always be said of me.

"Tanner, turn right here."

"Why? This is not the way to the nature preserve."

"Trust me."

"Do I have any other choice?"

Of course, he just smiled, his wrinkles bunching up like corduroy.

Two miles down the road, we came to a farm. *Change of venue for the nature talk?*, I wondered.

"Pull in front of the barn," Rigdon pointed as I pulled into the gravel driveway.

I parked my car next to an old tractor.

"Stay here." Rigdon jumped out and sauntered into the barn. Having no clue of his plans, I waited, recalling the great time I had at the camp. I thanked God and continued our conversation that began two days earlier. After a few minutes, Rigdon waved for me to join him in the barn. *Whatever*, I mused to myself.

"Ever ridden a horse?" the old man asked as we entered the building.

"What?!" I was astounded by the question and worried about what might follow.

"A horse," Rigdon said with a little sarcasm. "Have you ever ridden a horse?"

"That's what I thought you said," I replied, heading toward the barn door. "No, I've never ridden a horse. What happened to going to hear Dr. Maxwell?"

"We are. Here," he grabbed my arm and handed me the reins to a brown horse with a white patch on the underside of his neck. "Meet Mr. Henry, the bravest horse east of the Mississippi."

Rigdon mounted his horse. Still stunned by this unpredictable turn of events, I stood there motionless for several moments.

"Climb aboard."

*Yeah, right.* Like I knew how to mount a horse, let alone ride it. But, not wanting to look like a fool, I drew on my memories of watching Westerns as a child. *Foot in the hoop-thing, grab the handle of the saddle, and kick the other leg up and over the horse. One, two, three, go.*

Oomph! Not only did I not get on the horse, on the way back down, my foot slipped and I landed flat on my back on the barn

45

floor. By this time, Rigdon was laughing so hard he almost fell off his own horse.

I smiled, embarrassed, but determined. The second time was awkward, but successful.

"Rigdon, what are we doing here? Why are we on horses? What are you up to?"

"Follow me."

"How?"

"Just do what I do." A little kick in the side, followed by a whistling grunt, and his horse trotted out of the barn.

I followed suit, encouraging Mr. Henry to follow Rigdon. "Where are we heading?" I called to my tour guide.

"To the nature preserve."

And so we rode. It turned out that the lecture at the nature center didn't begin for another hour. So Rigdon had this horse thing planned from the beginning. But, as always, his plan would prove best.

I got the hang of horse riding quicker than I thought I would and soon we were chatting casually. But of course the small talk didn't last long.

"Is Christ the Treasure of your life?" Rigdon was ready to move onto deeper things. One minute we talked college football and the next minute he asked me about my relationship with God.

"Today, yes. Before the past two days, I'm not really sure." I knew he had set me up for something.

"Is Christ the Treasure of your Ministry Community?"

"I don't know. I hope so. I haven't really thought about it much. I mean . . . we talk about Him all the time."

"Christ must not only be the Treasure of your life as you know your Identity, develop Intimacy, and Integrate your faith . . . He must also be the Treasure of your ministry."

"What do you mean?"

"First, Christ must be the Treasure of your teaching time."

"Of course, I know that," I rebutted. Youth group existed so that we could help teenagers get to know God through Christ. Of course Christ was the Treasure of our teaching time.

"Here's what I mean. Many youth ministries today build around hot topics. We tell kids not to smoke, drink, have sex, and many other things. Tell me something, how many kids do you know at your church who don't know that those things are wrong?"

"Few, if any," puzzled as always by Rigdon's line of reasoning.

"Then why do many youth leaders spend all of their time telling kids that those activities are off limits? It's like trying to stop a bleeding artery with a band-aid. Too often we deal with symptoms instead of root causes."

Interesting point. I was guilty of the hot topic approach, but kids usually seemed excited and interested when we discussed those subjects.

"Do you know why most youth ministries use hot topics?" he adamantly asked.

I shrugged.

"Two reasons—parents want such topics, and kids enjoy them." Rigdon grew more intense as we rode side-by-side down the trail.

*Please the parents and the kids; what more could you ask for?* I wasn't about to tell Rigdon such a thought. I pulled on the reins. Mr. Henry must have been a well-trained horse because I did not have a clue about what I was doing.

"Parents want them because they want to protect their kids," Rigdon gently patted his horse. "Kids like them because it allows them to not really go deeper, or dig into the root causes of their behavior. In other words, it's much easier for everyone involved, including the youth leader. But . . ."

I could sense it coming now. Rigdon had a long way to go before he would convince me on this point. I was with him on the "Ministry Community" idea and the fact that Christ had to be the Treasure of my life, but no hot topics . . . that was a stretch.

"Rigdon," I interrupted, "Do you mean that we should never talk about those things?"

"That's not at all what I mean. Let me paint the picture for you," he pointed ahead on the trail. "Do you see that tree over there?"

"Yes." It was a monstrous giant oak, probably planted by Johnny Appleseed—if he planted oak trees. *Here it comes, the whole "plant your roots deep so you can grow tall" parable.*

"See the gray squirrel on the second branch?"

The old man caught me again. *If not the tree and roots thing, where is he going with this?*

"I see it," I answered

"See the birds flying to and from the tree?"

"Yeah." The nature lecture had already begun, with Rigdon playing the role of Dr. Maxwell.

"Why doesn't the squirrel just fly from tree to tree?"

*Okay, Pat, I risk $1000 on that question.* "Because he can't fly," I chuckled.

"How do you know that squirrels can't fly? How does he know that he can't fly? He doesn't fly because he's a squirrel. The temptation must be great for him to just fly from tree to tree. He must watch the birds and think, 'Wow, that looks like fun.' But, he doesn't fly . . . because he's a squirrel."

"If he tried to fly, he'd splatter all over the ground."

"True, but imagine the temptation . . . everyone else is doing it."

"What's your point?"

"He doesn't fly because he knows he's a squirrel. The core reason he does not fly is his understanding of who he is and who he is not . . . what he was created to be and what he was not created to be."

"Go on." He had gained my interest again.

"Christian teenagers face peer pressure every day to engage in sex, drugs, drinking, etc. . . But squirrels don't fly and when they try to, they splat all over the ground, as you say."

"Core reason, right?"

"Right. Don't teach them it's wrong to fly; squirrels already know that. Start at the core or the heart."

The nature preserve came into sight and boy was I happy to see it. My backside had already let me know that riding horses was not my thing.

"Rigdon, that sounds good, but where do I begin?"

"At the Source! You see, teaching about hot topics and other things that modify behavior, makes good kids, but it does not transform lives. If you're just interested in modifying behavior, protecting, and developing "good" kids who go on to college, get good jobs, have nice families, and don't do bad stuff, etc. . . you can use any materials you like. There are many, many books that will help you produce those types of kids."

"What's wrong with those types of kids? That is what parents want."

"But, Tanner, Christ doesn't call us simply to behavioral modification on the outside. He calls us to a transformation on the inside. Obedience to God should not be motivated by fear of punishment, but by love toward the One worth obeying."

"Wow, I guess you're right," I squirmed in my saddle. "That's a lot to consider all by itself. I have often found myself obeying out of guilt or fear of punishment, rather than love for my Lord Jesus Christ."

Rigdon nodded in agreement. "But it doesn't matter if I'm right or wrong, and that brings me back to my point. The only book I know of that God promises will transform lives is the Bible. If Christ is to be the Treasure of your Ministry Community, God's Word must be the source of your teaching."

"Okay. I'm with you."

"You must begin with Scripture and let the topics rise out of it, rather than imposing them upon it. Let God's Word speak to you where you are. It will, trust me, it will."

"I guess I need to make the Bible more a part of what we do on Sunday nights."

"Good start. Just remember the principle; if Christ is the Treasure of your Ministry Community, that must be reflected in your teaching."

"Gotcha. So I need to teach kids through the Bible about their Identity in Christ, how to develop Intimacy with Christ, and how to Integrate their faith into their lives. Right?" This was good stuff.

"You got it. The scary thing is that they will look more and more like you, so you'd better look more and more like Jesus. One more thing, I would challenge you to have your teenagers interact with God's Word. Don't just tell them about it. Let them look up passages, preferably in their own Bibles. They have to learn to use the mighty sword if they ever hope to survive on their own after leaving your care."

"I never thought of it that way. I guess I need to begin to think long-term about youth ministry. What am I preparing them to be? You know, I have a point for you, Rigdon, that I just thought of. We live the majority of our lives as adults, not as teenagers. There-fore, I need to be, more than anything else, training these young men and women to become adults after God's own heart."

"Bingo! Now you are catching on, my young friend. It won't be long before you're taking your own youth ministry student on a horse ride to the nature preserve," he said with a boisterous laugh.

# ⮞Chapter Seven⮜
## Ministry Design

We arrived at the nature center as they were beginning to serve lunch.

"Hungry?" Rigdon asked, as he pointed to a pavilion. A line of people had formed to fill their plates with food.

"Sure. Rigdon, do you know any of these people?"

"Yes, I come here every Saturday to hear Dr. Maxwell and share lunch and the Gospel with my nature friends."

What an amazing guy! I'd never met anyone like Rigdon before. Real . . . authentic, true, passionate, committed. I guess he reminded me of Jesus. The more I thought about it, he reminded me a lot of Jesus. With his veiled expressions and teaching side trips, he constantly gave me living parables . . . that he often had to explain. I felt like one of the bumbling disciples trying to understand the parables of Jesus.

Sure enough, we sat down next to some of Rigdon's friends and he immediately took up where he'd obviously left off last week . . . talking about Jesus. The shredded chicken sandwich and chips were enough to hold me over, but I really enjoyed the homemade vanilla-flavored root beer. We moved from the pavilion to tree-hewn benches set into the side of a hill, facing a small wooden stage in front of a row of trees. It looked like a pleasant setting . . . for a long nap.

"Ladies and Gentlemen, I'm proud to introduce our local nature expert, Dr. Kent Maxwell," an older gentleman addressed the group.

A smattering of applause erupted as a middle-aged man stepped onto the primitive stage in the natural amphitheater.

"Thank you. I would like to talk with you today about my friend the parrot." With a loud whistle he summoned a parrot, whose flapping wings just missed my head as he flew from the back of the crowd to the platform, coming to rest on the shoulder of the great doctor.

"Everyone . . . meet Francis. Francis . . . meet everyone."

"Hi everyone," Francis squawked. Laughter rose from the crowd.

"Francis can only repeat words said to her. She imitates sounds. She does not really understand words, but can imitate inflection and tone to make it sound like a word. She imitates the sounds around her. If she were in a cage with monkeys, she would begin to sound like a monkey. The same with cows or chickens or even laughing hyenas. She is an imitator."

"Imitator," Rigdon whispered in my ear. "Remember that . . . if Christ is to be the Treasure of your Ministry Community, He must be the Treasure of your life, your teaching, and your *Ministry Design*. Does your Ministry Design reveal Christ as the Treasure . . . or does it simply imitate its surroundings? Does your Ministry Design imitate culture or transform culture?"

Birds. Ministry Design. Vanilla root beer. Okay, maybe not the root beer, but God had a plan to put all this together somehow. Rigdon was the kind of guy who drove you nuts in the nicest way. Boy, did he make me think!

"What philosophy seems to be the god of this age?" he whispered again, before I even had time to consider his first question.

"Philosophy? I don't know."

"Hedonism. Fun. Does your Ministry Design imitate that cultural distinctive, or does it work to transform it?"

This was getting a little too deep for me. I wanted to get back to the parrot. Birds flying, making sounds, that was much easier to think about. Imitating a culture bent on hedonism with my Ministry Design? That was beyond me.

I spent the rest of Dr. Maxwell's presentation thinking about what Rigdon had said. *Does my Ministry Design imitate culture or transform it?* It really got to the heart of one of my biggest frustrations with youth ministry—the feeling that everything had to be entertaining. Seminars and conventions loaded me down with great game ideas and entertaining events. I felt tired of trying to "outdo" the competition from culture. They had the cash to entertain and I did not. I desperately wanted to see teenagers' lives transformed, not just give them momentary blips of happiness. *Uh, oh. Rigdon is leaning over again.*

"What are you saying to your youth about who God is and how He works, by your Ministry Design and methods?"

*He just never quits.* Our horse-riding trip to the nature preserve had become an informal seminar on youth ministry teaching and design. I was not complaining, but my brain started to hurt. These ideas were new to me and it was tough to process it all in the midst of Dr. Maxwell and his talking parrot, Francis. *My Ministry Design said something about God, but what?*

"Thank you, Dr. Maxwell," said the emcee as applause rose steadily from the crowd. "And thanks to all of you for joining us."

The trip back was easier than the one there. I became used to old Mr. Henry and it seemed he liked me. As the sun shone harshly on my neck in the open meadow, I sunk deep in thought.

*Ministry Design. How God works. Who God is. Wow! This is serious business.* Once again I squirmed in my saddle. *I thought youth ministry was just about finding a great game book, getting some snacks, teaching an interesting topic, developing relationships with teenagers, and maybe singing some worship songs. Now, I hear that even the way I do ministry reflects on who God is and how He works.* I felt the weight of responsibility bearing down on me.

"Polly want a cracker?" Rigdon broke the silence. "Hello. Are you in there?"

"Oh . . . yeah. I just drifted somewhere else, thinking about what you said earlier."

"Don't worry, the burden doesn't last long. Just long enough to make Christ the Treasure of not only *what* you do in your ministry, but also *how* you do it."

Rigdon always seemed to read my mind, share my burdens, and understand my feelings. I hoped that he was right. I needed resolution.

# ⌒Chapter Eight⌒
## Secret #3 . . . Team-Based Ministry

I spent the rest of Saturday watching football and preparing for youth group on Sunday. It had been nearly three months since I last prepared a youth meeting before Sunday afternoon. It felt good. I began to evaluate how we spent our time on Sunday evenings. How much of it was invested in our Treasure and how much of our time was just "spent"?

On Sunday night, I planned to talk about the Ministry Design of the New Testament from Acts 2:42–47. Again, I felt stumped as to the "how." Then I remembered the Team CE flyer. I went to the site www.teamce.com, and discovered that they offered a complete, simple, and easy youth program for a very minimal fee. And, the best part was that they seemed to know and understand the Secrets of the Simple Youth Ministry. I earnestly hoped that the teenagers would catch a glimpse of God's plan for us to create a Ministry Community together. We would begin the process of having a shared Treasure, Jesus Christ. For the first time in a long time, I felt excited about youth group.

It worked! Youth group went great. The changes were a bit strange for some. We did some team-building exercises from TeamCE instead of meaningless games. The crowd breaker fit right with the message instead of being disconnected. And I handed out daily and family devotionals for the teenagers to do throughout the week. They left with a fresh vision of what our ministry could become.

For the first week in nearly three months, I was flying high. I spent much of the week reading through the TeamCE Leader's Guide, trying to understand the model of ministry. I felt excited and I was pumped about the future of our ministry.

Friday night came and it was time for high school football. The Bulldogs were hot this season, 4-0. That night they would play against their nearby rivals. It would be an epic battle of two undefeated teams, with great implications for the league championship and beyond.

I got there early to see some of my kids play in the band before the game. I think they enjoyed seeing me there and I loved to watch them. The band was awesome, but Friday nights were about football, not the band. They knew it and so did the rest of the town.

*Wait a minute . . .* My mind started spinning again. *If Friday nights are about football, why does the band play? The answer is simple, student involvement. Uh, oh . . . I'm starting to think like Rigdon.* For the first time I realized that each student has different gifts and abilities; not all of them can play football. Some students love music and play in the band. Other students enjoy cheering for the team. Others twirl batons or wave flags or provide help in other areas. *The goal of the school is to get as many students involved as possible. Good idea.*

"Good evening, partner," Rigdon woke me from my private thoughts.

"Hey, Rigdon. I didn't know you came to the games," surprised to see my friend. "Have a seat."

"Fall Friday nights are about high school football. I wouldn't miss it, especially now."

I waited a few moments for him to explain his "especially now" comment. But, as I should have known, he wanted me to ask.

"What do you mean by 'especially now'?" *Here it comes, another teachable moment from the great master of simplicity.*

"You'll see in about . . ." He looked toward the giant scoreboard in the far end zone. "Oh . . . thirty-seven seconds."

"Rigdon, you always have something up your sleeve. By the way, Sunday night went great. I think I'm really starting to catch on to this whole Simple Youth Ministry thing. We talked about becoming a Ministry Community and stuff like that. It was cool; the kids actually paid attention."

"Sounds great, Tanner."

Bleeeeeep! Game time.

Our team had a huge kicker, about six foot two inches and two hundred and fifty pounds. His kick sailed to the two-yard line. The return was exciting for about three seconds. The runner juked left, cut right, found a seam at the twenty-yard line and took off.

Smash! You could hear the collision throughout the small stadium. Our kicker met the runner head-on at the thirty-five yard line. Play over. The crowd went wild, cheering for the home team.

Then, it happened. The play was over, but the kicking tee still rested on the forty-yard line. Usually a player or a ball boy will run out and pick up the tee. Not this time.

Silence engulfed the stadium as a young boy in a motorized wheelchair began to drive onto the field—Johnny Scruggs. I knew Johnny. Everyone loved him. Paralyzed from the waist down because of a tragic farming accident, he was a bright, handsome, but sometimes resentful, fifteen-year-old boy.

When the crowd recognized the wheelchair driver as Johnny, cheers filled with a deep sense of encouragement rose like a mushroom cloud from the stands. Johnny continued on toward his goal with the wind of the crowd's cheers pushing him along.

I will never forget that moment. It was not about Johnny's fifteen seconds of fame. It was not about the crowd feeling sorry for a boy scarred by tragedy. It was clearly about a love for Johnny. But the realization that captured me was that Johnny had a role and a responsibility. Just when everyone thought that he was useless, someone found a place for him to be useful.

When he arrived at the tee, he pulled out his grabber pole, reached out, captured the tee with its claws, and brought it into his lap. A successful trip. By the time he turned around to return to the bench, tee in hand, the crowd stood on its feet.

Tears began to well up in my eyes. Soon the visitors' stands were full of people standing, cheering for Johnny. Then the players on the sidelines, the players on the field, even the referees, caught up in the moment, began to cheer.

Johnny smiled, the biggest smile I had ever seen. He looked up at the crowd, grabbed the tee and raised it to the cheering fans as if to say "Thank you." People continued to clap and cheer until he reached the bench with the tee.

*Wow!* I took a deep breath as I sat down. The game continued, but I didn't notice. I remained captivated by the moment. *Incredible,* like nothing I had ever seen before.

Then I saw a magical connection. The head football coach turned toward the stands, surveying the crowd. His eyes locked on Rigdon as he flashed a thankful smile.

*Rigdon? The coach?* I glanced at Rigdon, to get his "take"on the event. He just smiled, a knowing smile. *Oh no . . . set up again.* I returned the smile.

"Did you have anything to do with this?" I asked.

"Moi?" he replied, his eyes revealing the satisfaction of a successful plan.

"Okay. What did you do? Go ahead . . . I know this is all about teaching me something."

"Yes, I would like to teach you something here, but it is not all about you. That is part of the point."

That stung, but I said, "I'm all ears."

"Johnny Scruggs, damaged, scarred for life, seen by some as a throwaway. Many kids you work with do not see their place in this world. They struggle with where they fit. What are their gifts, talents, and abilities and where can they use them?"

"I'm with you."

"Johnny, maybe now more than before his accident, needed a place to serve. I just spoke with Coach Billig about the possibility of making Johnny the tee fetcher. He asked Johnny at school today if he would be willing, and after a little encouragement, he agreed."

"You are the man! That was awesome."

"Don't miss the point here, Tanner."

"Go ahead."

"Remember, you mentioned that I probably wanted to teach you something here. You're right. But the first thing I'm trying to show you is that it is not about you." Rigdon pointed at me. "You immediately assumed that if I had something to do with Johnny, it was just for you."

*Double ouch!* He was right and I felt guilty.

"You see, many youth leaders see themselves as the 'show' for their youth ministry. One person doing all the work, getting all the glory, leaping tall buildings with a single bound."

"Super Me!" I knew that role.

"God's design for ministry is a team approach where everyone has a role and responsibility. That was my goal for Johnny; he needed to have a role beyond being a spectator."

Some of this sounded familiar from my reading of the TeamCE Leader's Guide. I repeatedly saw the value of a team approach to ministry.

"We all need to find our place, not just on a Friday night at a football game, but in life. Your kids need to find their place in your Ministry Community. Where can they serve? What role can they play to further the ministry? We give kids responsibility in every other area of life, except within the church. Youth leaders should blaze the path in making leaders out of teenagers."

"I'm listening. I know that we have way too many spectators in our church and our youth ministry. Too many people 'sitting the bench' and not involved. It's kind of like football. Twenty-two people do all the work on the field, while hundreds sit back and watch the show."

"You're catching on, Tanner. I believe that God's design for ministry is a team approach. Do you remember what Ephesians 4:12 talks about?"

"Yeah, it's the pastor's job to equip people to do ministry."

"Well . . ." Rigdon raised his eyebrows at me.

"I guess I've never really applied that to youth ministry. I've heard about having adult helpers and even student ministry teams, but never really about having all the students involved in leading and running the ministry."

"Let me warn you before you get too excited. Kids aren't always responsible. They often 'drop the ball' and don't do what they're supposed to do. They learn, however, from their failures and the rest of the group sees the need for accountability. Nonetheless, we must get them involved."

"So you're saying that I should give every teenager a role?"

"A *significant* role. And, do your best to help them identify their gifts and abilities first. Then let them choose the role best suited for them."

"What about teenagers who don't think they have talents and I can't really see their gifts either?"

"You mean like Johnny Scruggs?"

"Okay, I get your point. There's a place for everyone. If not, I guess I'll create one."

"The bottom line is that everyone needs to have a significant role that involves some level of decision-making. In other words, share the ministry with the teenagers."

"Okay, sounds good. Now I just have to figure out how to put this thing together."

"TeamCE."

"You know about TeamCE?" surprised, yet not shocked.

"Yeah, its origin comes from the first youth ministry movement in America, Christian Endeavor, started in 1881. Tried and tested, forgotten for years, but proven to work to develop young people into Christian leaders."

"I know, it's so cool. Come to think of it, I remember that it has stuff about doing the team ministry approach. You, Rigdon, are a wealth of information."

As always typical for me, I drifted deep into thought. *Team ministry? Sounds like a great idea.* Between watching a play here and there, I began thinking of ways to implement the team ministry approach.

*Josh would do well leading the Promotional/Publicity team. He is great for making flyers and getting the word out. He could bring his whole techno-geek crew onto his team and make it awesome. I didn't* even notice the game unless the crowd cheered, but still continued in my thoughts.

*Taylor loves people. She would be perfect for a Love/Welcome leader of friendly girls.*

My mind continued to wander as the gun sounded for the end of the first quarter. The score was tied 10 – 10. I remember the touchdowns, but I lingered deep in thought during the game. I usually meandered down to the north side of the field, where the students hang out after the first quarter. After a quick stop at the concession stand for a drink and a hotdog, I made my way to the sea of red and black. Everyone in the entire town seemed to wear the school colors for home games.

"Hey, Josh, how's it going?" I spotted one of the kids from my group. I did not understand why Josh and his gang came to the games. They disliked football. They were not in the band. They spent the entire game, every week, gathered together in their little group, eating junk food and talking about new software, new web sites or computer games. Although I claimed to be somewhat computer literate, I oftentimes had no clue what they talked about.

"Oh . . . Hi," Josh responded. "Did you see what they did with Johnny?"

"Yeah," I said, taken back by his question. Josh did not usually say much, let alone initiate a conversation.

"Wasn't that cool?" he said.

I nodded my head in disbelief. I had never been able to pull Josh out of his shell long enough to talk about things deeper than the latest computer game or software. This was exciting. *Rigdon . . . Was this another . . .?*

Josh continued, "I used to hang out with Johnny before his accident, but after he got hurt I just didn't know how to respond to him. I just felt like he was kind of useless now. It was really sad. But tonight . . . that was awesome."

"Yeah." Now was my opportunity. "Josh, where do you think you fit? I mean with our youth group and all. Do you feel useless?" I obviously caught him off guard. He had let his wall down and was now exposed.

"Uh . . . I've never really thought about it. I just come," the young man shifted from one foot to the other.

"What would you think about actually helping run youth group . . . as a team, rather than me doing everything?"

He acted a bit confused at first. "How?"

"What do you think you could do best as a part of the team?" I pointed toward him.

His eyes lit up and his countenance changed from his typical "whatever" attitude. The wheels began to turn as he chuckled, "Well . . . you know those flyers you send out to promote events. They're pretty corny sometimes. That clip art you use looks like the seventies or something. You have no consistency with your font presentation and your use of shading is completely inept."

I felt like a 15-year-old had just berated me, but swallowing my pride I said, "I guess I failed art."

"I just mean that when my friends get that stuff . . . they laugh."

"Alright, smart guy. Can you do better?"

"Well . . ."

"I guess we found your part on the team. You are in charge of promotion. Get your buddies to help you."

"But, I . . ."

"We have that hay ride coming up later this month. Do what you can to get the word out."

"How?"

"It's up to you. Call me if you have any questions. See ya."

I rushed out of there like Jerry running from Tom. I actually felt a little nervous about handing over some of my responsibilities. *What would the church say? What would parents say? I should probably have a talk with our pastor before I go too far with this team thing.*

We won the game by one point in double overtime. Everyone was excited, but the talk of the night was Johnny's triumphant entrance onto the field after every kickoff. And I will never forget the lessons I learned that night.

# ⤳Chapter Nine⤳
## Secret #4 . . . the Target

The youth group Sunday night had a great time. After my discussion with Rigdon at the football game and further reading in the teamce.com materials, I organized all our teams.

I could not remember a time when I had seen my teenagers so interested. Their eyes lit up when I talked about a team approach to the ministry and their possible roles and responsibilities. I guess this was the beginning of my students taking ownership of the ministry. Wow! Who would have thought that a simple shift in strategy would completely change our group?

"Rigdon. Hey, we had a great night tonight," I said, unable to control my enthusiasm as he entered the room following our youth meeting.

"That's great. I heard kids plotting their roles on each team as they came down the hallway. Sounds like you struck a chord."

"Amazing! Why isn't everyone doing this?"

"I don't know. It seems simple enough."

"I think we're finally on the right track."

"Oh yeah . . . what track is that?" Rigdon spoke with a growing smirk, reminiscent of his entrée to sharing a new "secret" with me.

"Now what?" I laughed. Fully prepared, in fact, excited to learn more.

"Well, where are you heading?"

"Home," I said.

"Tanner, sometimes you're a tough one," Rigdon rolled his eyes. "Not 'where you're heading right now.' Where is your ministry heading?"

"Oh . . . yeah . . . I knew that's what you were getting at," I said, smiling at Rigdon's laughter. *Time for me to clue in.* "Well, Rigdon. I . . . We . . . well we . . . I'm trying to help kids come to Christ and follow Him." It sounded weak, but true. He had me right where he wanted me.

"Meet me at my house tonight at midnight."

"Midnight? Why?"

"Midnight. Come prepared to sleep under the stars. See you later."

*What a strange bird! Midnight . . . sleep under the stars . . . weird. Oh, well . . . nothing to lose . . . except maybe sleep. But everything to gain.*

I gathered my sleeping bag, a small tent, my official "Ranger Mark Backpack," and my monster flashlight for the midnight adventure. I prepared for anything Rigdon might throw at me. I had learned to expect the unexpected.

After packing my car, I headed to Rigdon's place on the other side of town. He lived next to the area state park in a little two-bedroom house with a two-foot-high white picket fence surrounding the yard. It was quaint, maybe too quaint. It made me nervous when situations seemed too perfect. When I arrived, Rigdon stood in the garage.

"Welcome," he said. "Welcome to the final piece of the *Simple Youth Ministry* picture." He was packing some supplies into a basket on the rear of a four-wheeler. *A four-wheeler?*

"Rigdon, what's up with the four-wheeler?"

"Transportation."

"Where are we going?"

"I reveal no secret before its time. Put your stuff in the basket and let's go."

After a few minutes of forcing my equipment into the small basket, we headed off. Rigdon drove and I sat directly behind him holding on for dear life. He may have been an old man, but he was not afraid of speed. Soon we flew through a vast meadow, heading straight for the park. As we neared the entrance, Rigdon turned to speak.

"I know the park manager. We went to grade school together. He allows me to come and enjoy the park after it's closed. Don't ever forget the importance of relationships." Always the teacher, he could not avoid the opportunity to pass on another nugget.

Once inside the park, Rigdon chose a trail and began climbing a hill through the dark. Although the four-wheeler had headlights, visibility was not good. The harder it was to see, the faster he drove. Rigdon always stood on the verge of crazy lunatic and wise guru on my score sheet. Now he was crossing the line.

"We'll be getting off here," Rigdon called back to me.

I looked around to gauge the area . . . dark, too dark for me, were my sentiments. Although the moon was full this time of year, we were deep in the woods and shielded by trees. Soon we headed off, walking along the trail by foot. I had my backpack with my sleeping bag and other supplies. Rigdon carried a strange contraption on his back. It looked like a large rectangular aluminum case with straps. It was old, scratched and army green. I decided not to ask. In the meantime, I found my monster flashlight, clicked it on, and suddenly felt safe.

"Please turn off the flashlight and be quiet."

"What? It's pitch black."

"Follow me, Tanner. I know the way."

*Unbelievable. Midnight. Four-wheeler. Middle of the woods. No flashlight. Was I stupid, or what? I could be home catching some Z's—instead I am out here in the middle of nowhere following some guy who finds joy in living out the X-Files.* I kept my complaining to myself.

We followed a trail heading up to what appeared to be a mountaintop. Soon the moon broke through the tree cover, lighting our path. Rigdon had a plan . . . I had no other option but to trust him. There was no turning back now. I would get lost if I decided to go back on my own, flashlight or no flashlight.

"Whoa!!" My foot slipped on the edge of a stone outcropping and I fell at least ten feet straight down into a pit. "Ouch!" I landed on my feet only to fall backward onto my backside. I immediately reached for my flashlight as I yelled at Rigdon. "Can I use my flashlight now?" I screamed.

"I should warn you, there will be some pitfalls along the way."

There was Rigdon waxing philosophical as I sat submerged in a fern-filled pit with who knows how many strange creatures crawling all over me.

As I surveyed my situation with my flashlight, I began to laugh . . . more out of embarrassment than joy. The pit was only three feet deep at the most. There would be no need for a mountainside rescue unit. I simply crawled out as Rigdon stood laughing hysterically. It may have been pitch dark, but I was sure he could see me blushing. It seemed he always got the upper hand.

We hiked on and on, up the mountain, through dirt, stones, brush, and over little streams. I tried to strike up a conversation a few times but Rigdon rebuffed with a, "Shhh . . . Listen . . . Look around."

I had always appreciated the outdoors, but I certainly enjoyed the comforts afforded by twenty-first century technology. I suppose I had not taken much time to really "smell the flowers" or take in the beauty of God's creation. I thought, *That must be Rigdon's plan; creation teaches us something about youth ministry.* If that were the case, I would much prefer daylight so I could really enjoy the beauty.

After about an hour of hiking, we reached what appeared to be the summit.

"This is it," my great and wise guru said with a sense of accomplishment and satisfaction.

"Okay . . . what do we do now?"

"Have a seat . . . over there on that big rock."

"Okay. Am I allowed to talk now?"

"Yes, of course," he said. He seemed amazed that I would even ask a question like that.

I threw my gear down and plopped down on the rock. *How was I supposed to know the rules here?*

The old man didn't stop to rest, but began to unpack his aluminum case as I sat thinking of what to ask first.     "So, why the trip in the dark?"

"Tanner, how did you feel walking through the woods in the dark?"

"Insecure and uneasy. It was tough, not knowing the path."

"And your teenagers . . . do they know the path? Do they know where they're heading?"

I should have known it all along. The darkness, no flashlight, follow the leader. Rigdon remained poised to enlighten me to the principles of providing godly direction to my teenagers.

"You are a tricky man, Rigdon. Yes, it was very tough in the darkness. And you're saying that my teens walk through the world on a path that they have never been on before."

"More than that my friend. I was your guide. I was your light for the path." He continued to finagle the aluminum case. After it opened, he assembled what appeared to be a tripod.

"So I should help guide teenagers along the path of life, right?"

"Yes, but there is more," he answered.

Yep, it was a tripod, or an easel. *That's an easel to hold a canvas for painting. Painting?* The moon was bright, but certainly not bright enough for painting. I didn't reveal my puzzled thoughts, but said, "Go on. I'm listening."

"I knew where I wanted to take you. I had a plan for our destination . . . a target. Do you have a target for your youth ministry?" he continued working. "In other words, do you know where you want your teenagers to end up? What do you want them to look like when they leave your ministry?"

"Uh . . . well . . . I want them to look like Jesus."

That seemed like a good answer. What youth worker does not want his or her teenagers to look like Jesus? Rigdon did not respond for what seemed like five minutes as he continued to assemble his contraption. It began to take form as he pulled a canvas over a makeshift frame that he unfolded from the aluminum case. He began to staple the canvas to the frame. *Amazing . . . I actually think he is going to paint out here in the middle of nowhere, in the dark, at 1:30 in the morning.* "Hello . . . Rigdon. Are you still with me?"

"Jesus?"

"Yes, Jesus. I want them to look like Jesus."

"Good. What does Jesus look like?"

*Wow! What a question!* Adjectives raced through my mind as I tried to come up with just a few that would capture the life of Jesus. He was certainly kind and compassionate, loving and caring. Yet, He was also direct and blunt, serious and committed.

As I pondered Rigdon's question, he continued to remove supplies from his mysterious case. He had an easel set up, a canvas on a frame resting on the easel, and then began to pull out paints and brushes. Sure enough, he was going to paint—*or . . . ask me to paint. No way,* I thought.

"You think about your target, what you want your teenagers to look like by the time you're done with them. I'll paint."

"Paint? In the dark?"

"I'm painting what *will* be in just a few short hours. I'm painting what I will see."

This guy started to sound more and more like some mystic from the desert. But, what could I do? I laid out my bedding on the mountaintop as I continued to think through his question.

*What did I want my teenagers to look like when they entered the adult world? What would it look like for them to be men and women after God's heart?* Slowly my mind began to drift as I climbed into my sleeping bag. Without any caffeine to carry me through, I drifted off to dreamland.

*The smell of greasy fries and elephant ears drew me deep into my dream world. I found myself walking the midway at the county fair. People smiled and laughed, ate and enjoyed themselves. It was a joyous occasion. Every stand seemed busy, as unwitting pawns waltzed through Vanity Fair.*

*One booth stood empty except for a man in his thirties sitting on a stool sketching a picture. I moved in closer to catch a glimpse of his sketch. There was no customer to be found, but he continued to draw.*

*It was a portrait of a young adult graduating from high school wearing a cap and gown. The surrounding noise grew quiet as I drew closer to the picture.*

*"My son," the man muttered. He turned to me. I saw tears rolling slowly down his cheeks.*

*"I remember the day he was born. I could not stop crying tears of joy for the gift God had given me. Now I cry tears of joy for the man he became."*

*I stared patiently at the picture, waiting for the story to continue, afraid to meet eyes with the man in his pain—curious to know how a man so young could have a boy so old.*

*"The day he was born, I had a picture in my mind of what I prayed he would look like as a young man. I wanted him to be passionately in love with Jesus. I wanted him to look like Jesus in the way that Jesus treated people and laid down His life for others so that God would be glorified. Francis lived my prayers out.*

*"He was a boy who loved life. At an early age, he trusted Christ as His Savior. Although he had his ups and downs, he followed Jesus with everything. His life verse was 'to live is Christ and to die is gain.' He lived it.*

*"He looked like Jesus. He was special."*

*Sincerity gushed from his heart as he continued the story. By now, tears filled my eyes and were overflowing.*

*"On the night before his high school graduation, he put his life on the line for his enemy. He was downtown with some friends, having some pizza and just hanging out when he heard some commotion outside the pizza place. Downtown is not very safe at night."*

*His eyes began to light up as he continued.*

*"Francis and his friends went outside to see what was happening. As it turns out, a kid who had continually picked on him for his faith at school, was being harassed by an older group of troublemakers. Francis, being the peacemaker Jesus asks us to be, stepped in.*

*"The gang of older kids threatened to kill Francis if he didn't get out of the way. Then he said it . . . the words any Christian parent fears, yet hopes their child would have the courage to say. Francis looked right into the eyes of that older group of kids and said, 'I'm not afraid to die. I have trusted Jesus Christ to save me from the punishment for my sins and to give me eternal life. I am free to die because I know where I'm headed. Now please leave these kids alone.'*

*"Adults and kids alike were stunned in the crowd that had gathered. Here was a young man willing to lay his life on the line. No fear of death."*

I could almost hear the words of Paul saying, "O death, where is thy sting."

*"My Francis had become a man after God's heart, willing to lay down his life, completely and utterly committed to following Christ."*

I was a bit confused at this point. Was Francis dead? Did they kill him? If not, why was this man crying? Then it really got weird.

A little boy climbed up on the chair where the person getting sketched usually sits.

*"Hi Francis, how's my little boy today?"* the artist said. *"I'm still sketching what you will become."*

# Chapter Ten
## The Midnight Sunrise

"Whoa! Get off me." I awoke to find a spider attempting to climb into my nostrils. I quickly jumped up, only to find Rigdon positioned in front of his canvas still painting in the dark. The sun started to show signs of peeking over the horizon.

"Rigdon, what are you still doing up?"

"Painting."

*Creative answer,* I smirked inside. "What are you painting?"

"The sunrise."

*Was I still dreaming or did he say, the sunrise? The sun was not even up yet. How could he possibly be painting the sunrise?* I moved closer to get a better view of his painting.

Sure enough . . . it was a beautiful sunrise, at least what I could see of it. I will never forget what happened during the next few minutes. As the sun continued to make its way over the horizon, I could see more and more of Rigdon's painting.

*Amazing. Awesome.* I could not believe my eyes. The picture unfolding in the skies also stood right in front of my face in matching hues on a canvas. Rigdon had captured the sunrise even before it happened . . . in the dark!

"What? . . . How? . . . Rigdon!"

"Relax. I'm not a prophet or anything. I've been up here many nights to take in the sunrise. I see it best in the night before it happens."

"I would say so . . . man, you drive me nuts. You are so strange."

"I am an artist. Artists see what they want their painting to become *before* they begin," he wiped his paint brush with a rag. "You, my friend, are a Youth Ministry Artist."

"Youth Ministry Artist?"

"You must learn to see what you want your kids to look like before you pick up the brush and choose your colors. You must have the end product in mind before you begin."

"Youth Ministry Artist?" I asked. "But God does the real painting here."

"Exactly, but He uses us. Let His Mighty Hand direct your hand on the canvas. He will help you choose the perfect hues. He will give you the vision for what your teenagers are to become; just seek Him."

"I had this dream while you were painting," I said.

"Let me guess . . . Francis?"

"No way! How did you know?" This was getting more mysterious every moment. Now he knew what I was dreaming? Impossible.

"Actually, I just heard you say Francis in your sleep. Gotcha," he said with his knowing smile.

"Whoa, I was starting to think you were an angel or something like that. Anyway, he talked about the same idea. Starting with the end in mind. A target to shoot at."

"Right. You want your kids to look like Jesus. What did He look like? A good Youth Ministry Artist will see the painting in his mind first."

"I don't have much of an imagination."

"Close your eyes and ask God to show you some things you've learned throughout Scripture that will help give you a picture of the kind of disciples you would like to develop."

I took a few minutes of silence to seek an answer from God, but it was not working. I heard no divine voice calling out the answers. My impatience kicked in.

"Rigdon, I don't know. It just doesn't seem to be coming."

"Get your stuff and let's head back down the mountain," he said.

We left. I felt a little disappointed, but my mind raced. Again, Rigdon had opened the floodgates for me. A simple trip through the dark. A weird dream. A strange portrait of a sunrise before it happened. *Somehow God uses this stuff.*

# ⤖Epilogue⤕
## Becoming a Youth Ministry Artist

I cancelled youth group for the coming Sunday night and told parents and kids that I would not be available all week. With Rigdon's help, I convinced the park ranger to let me spend the week in a tent on the top of the mountain. I quickly began to question my own psychological makeup after deciding to camp out for a week.

My Bible, my God, and me. One week of seeking God's portrait for my youth ministry. What did He want these teenagers to look like by the time they left my care? I even brought Rigdon's aluminum case, set up the easel, and put a canvas on it. I knew nothing about painting, but maybe God would show me.

At the bottom of the canvas Rigdon had given me were the words, Humility, Integrity, and Truth. Always the teacher, he gave me a place to start. I began to search the Scriptures and the Biblical portrait of Jesus for answers. Before the week ended, God had painted a picture for me—a beautiful portrait of a follower of Christ. I now had my target.

Sunday came and I couldn't wait to get to church to tell Rigdon about my great plans for the youth ministry. I showed up early to meet with, and pray for, our Senior Pastor before the service. Normally every Sunday morning at 8:00 a.m. sharp, Rigdon waits for me at the door. Not this Sunday; he was nowhere to be found.

"Pastor, have you seen Rigdon?"

"He and his mother moved to some little town over the weekend. I think they said Willard, Ohio or something like that. He said something about someone else in another town needing to learn the Secrets. I don't know what he was talking about. He was always a little strange to me."

"Strange indeed," I said with a knowing smile, the one I inherited from my friend and mentor. "I sure will miss him."

After prayer and Sunday school, the service began. I led the worship services that morning. After leading the music, I sat down to listen to the sermon.

"Our text for today is Acts 2:42–47," Pastor began, "The sermon is entitled, "Creating a Ministry Community.""

I chuckled to myself, *Rigdon must have rubbed off on the Senior Pastor.*

As I turned in my own Bible to follow along, a folded sheet of paper fell out. *Rigdon . . . that guy never quits.*

**Dear Youth Ministry Artist,**

**Do not hide the Secrets of the Simple Youth Ministry. Spread them far and wide.**

**For Christ and His Church,**

**Rigdon**

**P.S. Practice mounting a horse before you take your student to the Nature Preserve.**

Although Tanner was a fictional character, he struggled with the same desires, hopes, and issues of most youth leaders. The following pages include questions and tools for you to think about and apply to your own ministry. Who knows? Maybe someday you will be riding a horse teaching someone else the *Secrets of the Simple Youth Ministry*.

For more information go to www.teamce.com where you will find the secrets of the simple youth ministry put into action.

# MINISTRY COMMUNITY

*Acts 2:42–47*

*They devoted themselves to the apostles' teaching and to the fellowship, to the breaking of bread and to prayer. Everyone was filled with awe, and many wonders and miraculous signs were done by the apostles. All the believers were together and had everything in common. Selling their possessions and goods, they gave to anyone as he had need. Every day they continued to meet together in the temple courts. They broke bread in their homes and ate together with glad and sincere hearts, praising God and enjoying the favor of all the people. And the Lord added to their number daily those who were being saved.*

1. List the things that show the early church was a community.

2. What was the main element that brought the believers together?

3. Picture some of the members of your youth group in the above setting. What would be the different reactions to such a group?

4. Why do you think that the Lord "added to their number daily?"

5. Look at your list in question #1. List specific ways that these things could be lived out in your group today. For instance, how could your teens "have all things in common?"

# THE ESSENTIAL I'S

*1 Corinthians 2:7*

*No, we speak of God's secret wisdom, a wisdom that has been hidden and that God destined for our glory before time began.*

1. What things did Tanner struggle with in leading his youth group?

2. How did he try to solve these problems?

3. Read Philippians 2:21. How does this passage relate to the frustration that Rigdon felt toward many Christians? Does this passage apply to your group?

**IDENTITY**

*How great is the love the Father has lavished upon us that we should be called children of God. And that is what we are.* 1 John 3:1

1. Where did Rigdon tell Tanner to find his identity?

2. Why is finding your identity in Christ so important?

3. What have you found your identity in up until now? What can you do to change that?

## INTIMACY

*O LORD, you have searched me and you know me.* Psalm 139:1

1. God desires intimacy with us. How did Rigdon tell Tanner to gain intimacy with God?

2. Thinking back to the first church or ministry community, in what ways did the believers demonstrate that they had intimacy with God?

3. What areas in your own life and ministry lack intimacy? Explain.

## INTEGRATION

*So whether you eat or drink or whatever you do, do it all for the glory of God.* 1 Corinthians 10:31

1. Why is it important to integrate your faith in every aspect of your life?

2. How does the lack of integration in your life affect your ministry?

3. How have you "compartmentalized" your own life? What steps could you take to integrate your faith into these compartments?

# TREASURE

*Matthew 6:21*

*For where your treasure is, there your heart will be also.*

Take some time to be alone with the Lord to examine your heart and relationship with Him.

1. Honestly describe your relationship with God.

2. What would your family, friends, co-workers, and teenagers say is the treasure of your life?

3. What things in your life occupy your time and thoughts?

4. Describe your hunger for God.




5. What could you change to make God the Treasure of your life?

# CHRIST AS THE TREASURE OF YOUR MINISTRY & TEACHING

*2 Timothy 3:16–17*

*All Scripture is God-breathed and is useful for teaching, rebuking, correcting, and training in righteousness, so that the man of God may be thoroughly equipped for every good work.*

1. What did Rigdon say must be the SOURCE of our teaching?

2. How can you get God's Word to rise out of your teaching?

3. List some ideas for getting your teens to INTERACT with God's Word.

## TREASURE OF YOUR TEACHING

1. What did Rigdon call "hot topics" for youth group?
How do teens usually respond to these topics?

2. Is it difficult for you to let go of these types of curriculum and topics? Why or Why not?

3. Stop and think about each teen in your group. What lies at the "core" of each one? What motivates, tempts, or encourages them?

# CHRIST AS THE TREASURE OF MINISTRY DESIGN

*Romans 12:2*

*Do not conform any longer to the pattern of this world, but be transformed by the renewing of your mind.*

Now evaluate your present ministry.

1. How does your ministry IMITATE culture? What activities and curriculum do you use in your program that imitate the culture?

2. How did the first church TRANSFORM the culture around it?

3. What things could you change in your program that would cause your group to stop "imitating" and begin "transforming?"

Use the following chart to evaluate the time spent or invested in your present ministry. *Ministry Community Time Invested or Spent*

*Outline your weekly Ministry Community meeting:*

| **TIME** | **ACTIVITY** | **SPENT or INVESTED** |
|---|---|---|
| *7:00–7:05* | *Announcements* | *Spent* |

*Time Spent =*
     *vs.*
*Time Invested =*

1. What do you think your current Ministry Community structure communicates to your teenagers about what is important?

2. What would you like them to see as important?

# MINISTRY DESIGN ESSENTIALS

*Acts 2:42*

*They devoted themselves to the apostles' teaching, to the fellowship, to the breaking of bread, and to prayer.*

Design your own ministry using the first church as a model. Under each component, list things you would like to see happen in your youth group.

1.      Apostles' Teaching


2.      Fellowship


3.      Breaking of Bread


4.      Prayer

# TEAM MINISTRY

*Philippians 1:4–5*

*In all my prayers for all of you, I always pray with joy because of your partnership in the gospel from the first day until now . . .*

1. What have been the roles of the leaders and teenagers within your group?

2. List all the roles and needs of your group. Decide how you can give each member a significant role to fulfill these needs.

3. How can you involve everyone in your group in decision-making at some level?

4. Spend some time thinking about what you expect out of your teens based on their abilities, age-levels, and maturity. Outline a simple system for progressive responsibility for the members of your group. How do you plan to raise them up in making decisions, significant roles, and responsibility as they mature spiritually, physically, and emotionally?

**SHARED MINISTRY WORKSHEET**

| Teenagers | Role | Possible Future Responsibilities |
|-----------|------|----------------------------------|
| 1. | | |
| 2. | | |
| 3. | | |
| 4. | | |
| 5. | | |
| 6. | | |
| 7. | | |
| 8. | | |
| 9. | | |
| 10. | | |
| 11. | | |
| 12. | | |
| 13. | | |
| 14. | | |
| 15. | | |

# TARGET

*Philippians 1:21*

*To live is Christ and to die is gain.*

Paint the picture of what you want your teenagers to look like when they leave your care.
* List qualities, attributes, passions, etc...
* What qualities of Christ do you wish for them to imitate?

To order additional copies of

Have your credit card ready and call

**Toll free: (877) 421-READ (7323)**

or send $9.99 each plus
Shipping & Handling*

Your Choice: $3.95 - USPS 1st Class
$2.95 - USPS Book Rate

to
**WinePress Publishing
PO Box 428
Enumclaw, WA 98022**

www.winepresspub.com

*Add $1.00 S&H for each additional book ordered.